FOYLE'S HASTINGS

THE OFFICIAL INVESTIGATION

D1198850

Welcome to Foyle's Hastings

This is your official guide to the many Hastings locations made famous by the popular ITV detective show.

The show has proved incredibly popular both at home and abroad, with many fans being inspired to visit the town.

Use this guide to discover the special relationship that can sometimes exist between the reality of a place and the fiction of a television programme.

INVESTIGATION DEPARTMENT: List of Evidence Page

Evidence (i)

Proof of filming
in Croft Road,
Hastings

There is no doubt that Hastings has proved a successful setting for Foyle's War. Greenlit Rights, the show makers, have returned to film every series in the town, and each has seemed to be more popular than the last. It was 2001 when the Foyle's War team first moved into the streets of the Old Town to make the pilot episode, since then they returned regularly to transport Croft Road and the surrounding area back to the 1940s. Like the success of Hastings as a film location, the popularity of Foyle's War with TV viewers is indisputable. Episodes typically attract more than nine million viewers on ITV1 in the UK, with many more millions watching worldwide. Viewers enjoy following Foyle's meticulous investigations and appreciate the show's gentle tension and mystery. Although other locations have been used, the illusion of the show being completely based in Hastings is never spoiled.

Although we now believe the final episodes have beens shot, set after peace returned to Hastings, the show is regularly repeated on television here. Indeed, Foyles War is popular around the world.

Following the successful first and second editions this newer updated guide provides even more for Foyle's fans. Read on for the latest exclusive behind-the-scenes photos, a deeper look into wartime Hastings and an interview with the show's creator Anthony Horowitz.

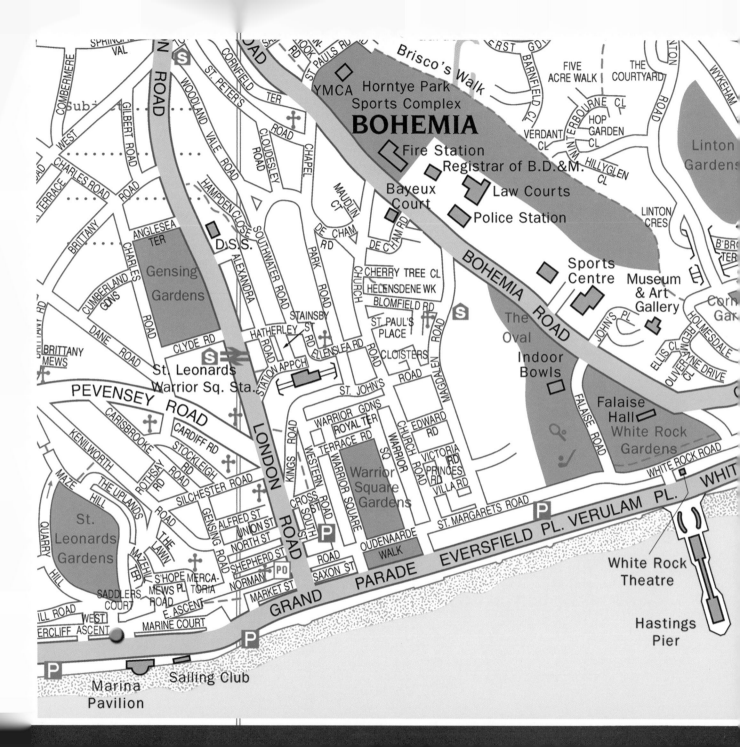

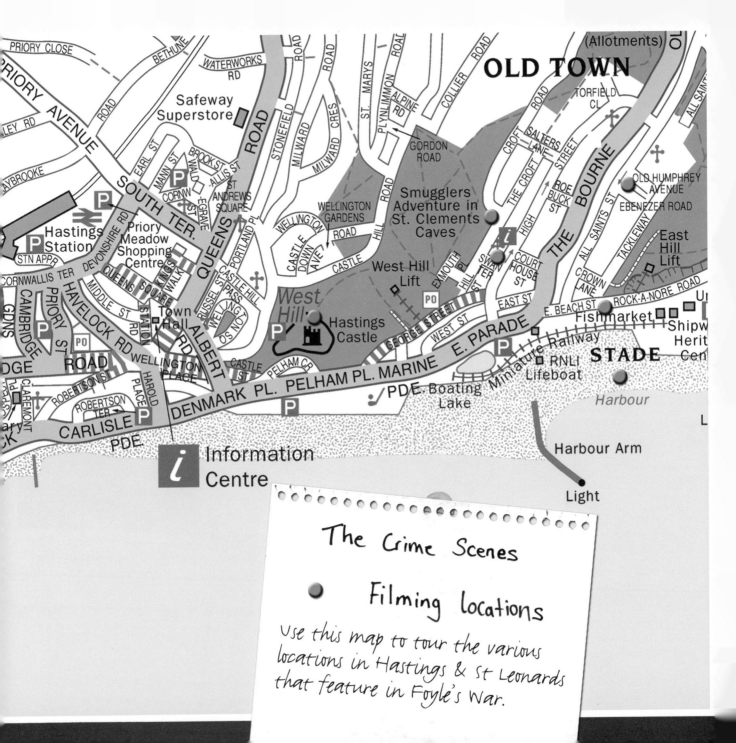

Information Centre

The Crime Scenes

● Filming locations

Use this map to tour the various locations in Hastings & St Leonards that feature in Foyle's War.

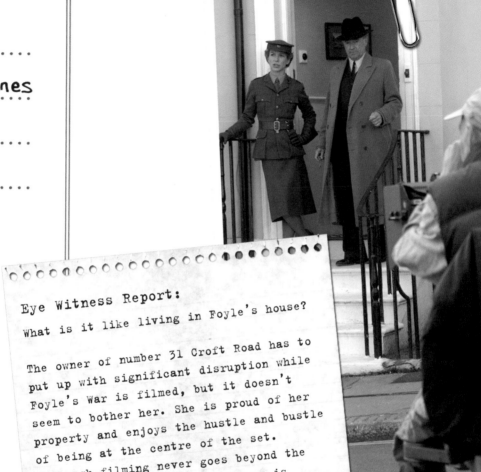

Eye Witness Report:

What is it like living in Foyle's house?

The owner of number 31 Croft Road has to put up with significant disruption while Foyle's War is filmed, but it doesn't seem to bother her. She is proud of her property and enjoys the hustle and bustle of being at the centre of the set. Although filming never goes beyond the entrance to number 31, the owner is restricted from entering and leaving her house at certain times and outside filming season a trail of Foyle's fans flock to the house to see it off screen. However, there are some hidden benefits, meeting the stars and getting to know the plot months in advance!

INVESTIGATION DEPARTMENT: Crime Scenes

Surveillance has uncovered filming activity in the following locations.

1. Location: Croft Road

Known as Steep Street on screen, Croft Road is where much of the filming action takes place. The road's distinctive architecture and intimate feel make it an ideal home for Detective Chief Superintendent Christopher Foyle, who lives at number 31. The striking front is instantly recognisable from the numerous times it is shown when DCS Foyle enters or leaves.

Croft Road is far from an ideal film location. It is a winding and narrow street, with poor access from surrounding Old Town roads. Although this may put most producers off, the makers of Foyle's were won over by its charm and decided to overcome these logistical difficulties. The road is closed during filming and access from surrounding areas is restricted. The film crew has to get used to working in confined conditions, and relies on the cooperation of residents, police and the local authority with road closures and traffic restrictions.

Hill Street, Church Passage and Post Office Passage, which run off Croft Road and the High Street are also used in episodes. Typical Old Town twittens, these are narrow, atmospheric streets that create the intensity perfect for Foyle's War.

Subject.........
Crime Scenes

....

....

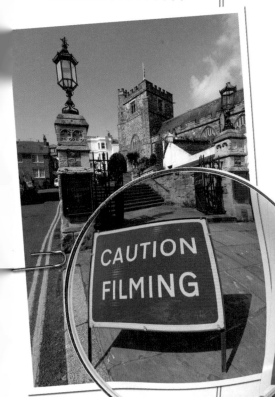

CAUTION FILMING

2. Location: Swan Terrace

This small terrace runs next to St Clements Church off High Street. The church appears every time Honeysuckle Weeks' character, Sam, drives up to the house where DCS Foyle lives in the show. The church was also used in a scene where DCS Foyle and Sam are together on the National Day of Prayer.

At the bottom of Swan Terrace is a memorial garden where The Swan Inn once stood before it was destroyed in an enemy air raid during the Second World War.

In one episode of the show, DCS Foyle drives down Swan Terrace past the memorial gardens. Although the episode is set in 1940, the Swan Inn was not destroyed until three years later. In reality in 1940, Christopher Foyle would have passed a very different scene at the bottom of Swan Terrace to that which can be seen today.

Locals get involved

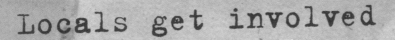

Hastings fishermen were used as extras to help in the recreation of the Dunkirk evacuation in series one. Local fisherman Graham Bossom's boat took the role of Lady Rose. Graham and fellow fishermen were caught up in the action, taking parts as extras. They physically launched and recovered a fishing boat using old fashioned methods, and also played parts as wounded soldiers. Hastings fishermen did indeed take part in the Dunkirk evacuation as did the Hastings lifeboat. This dramatic event was re-enacted on Hastings beach, bringing home the disturbing horror of the Dunkirk evacuation.

Evidence that local suspects were involved.

3. Location: The Stade

Hastings' fishing beach, or the Stade as it is known locally, has been used by Foyle's War crews in several episodes. Besides being an authentic fishing beach, and home to fishermen who adhere to traditional beach launched fishing methods, the Stade is an atmospheric and attractive piece of beach, the perfect setting for Foyle's War drama.

The name Stade comes from the Saxon word meaning 'landing place' and has been used for this part of Hastings' beach for a thousand years. In fact Hastings is now home to the largest beach launched fishing fleet in Europe.

Film crews overcame the obstacles of a working beach to film some very dramatic scenes, including a moving reconstruction of the Dunkirk evacuation, a stabbing, and a marriage proposal. The harbour arm, which was never properly completed, was used in series five in scenes involving DCS Foyle and Sam. The Stade was used for night shoots in series one and five for some intense scenes after dark, which required floodlights and other equipment to be brought in.

4. Location: The Net Huts

These historic buildings were another example of how Hastings fishing heritage was used. They featured heavily in the episode 'The German Woman' during a tense chase sequence. The net huts are distinct landmarks and are unique to Hastings. Fishermen used these tall shed-like buildings to store their nets in.

The weather boarded and tarred structures date from the 19th century. At this time, space was at a premium, so the huts were made as tall as possible to give fishermen enough space.

5. Location: The Pier

Rubber barbed wire was set up on the beach for a scene beneath the Pier in an early episode. As with most piers, Hastings was sectioned during the Second World War for fear of German invasion, cutting off the main pier structure from the shore promenade. Although suffering some bomb damage, the pier was reopened in 1946.

First opened in 1872, the Pier was once home to three halls, the Pier Pavilion, the Pier Theatre and a bandstand.

The Pier had a particularly lively role during the 1920s and 30s. During this period Hastings Pier provided much entertainment. There was dancing every night, daytime concerts, stunt diving, and speedboat trips out to the harbour and back.

Sadly Hastings Pier was very badly damaged by fire on 5th October 2010.

6. Location: The Royal Victoria Hotel, St Leonards

One of the town's most historic and striking buildings, this hotel was used by the Foyle's War crew in the episode 'Eagle Day' when DCS Foyle and Detective Sergeant Milner are called to investigate a stabbed body found in the aftermath of a bombing raid. During the filming for this episode, the A259 outside the hotel, one of the UK's busiest roads, had to be temporarily closed.

Originally known as the St Leonards Hotel it was renamed after Queen Victoria's patronage and her signature can still be seen in the Visitors' Book.

The hotel was the flagship building in Burtons' St Leonards, the new seaside town built by James Burton, after he bought the parish in 1828. Burton based his designs for St Leonards closely on his ideas and experiences at Regents Park, London. At the time, the medical profession had begun to report the health benefits of living by the sea, so more and more wealthy people chose to visit the seaside. Burton's vision was to create an elegant seaside town to cater for the health and recreational needs of wealthy and influential visitors.

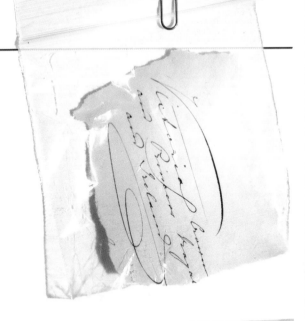

Subject.........

Deception and

Disguise.....

..

Wartime Britain is eerily recreated in a modern residential area of Hastings Old Town. How does the Foyle's War crew manage to transform our modern town so accurately?

1.   Designers have to hide or remove every single trace of the 21st century. This includes the smallest item that would escape the notice of most people. Meticulous attention to detail is required to ensure that yellow lines, parking meters, TV aerials, satellite dishes and burglar alarms are all removed or concealed. Road markings are temporarily covered with gravel and modern PVC window frames are covered with black tape. Removable items like street signs and satellite dishes are taken away and anything that can't be moved gets a clever disguise. Black adhesive covering is stuck over large areas of glass to hide double-glazing and some house fronts are boarded up to look like a wartime bomb blast defence. Shop fronts are redressed with period products and adverts swapped for popular products of the time.

2.   Modern streetlights are concealed using Victorian-style lamppost covers and bollards are covered in a similar way. Period cars are used to hide things in the road that can't be moved and newspaper stands cover up other modern day give-aways. Modern houses are painted in a bigger range of brighter colours than they were, so designers try to hide the most extravagant colours, keeping closer to the muted, sombre colours of the 40s.

3.   Costume designers and make-up artists are on set to ensure characters fit in with the authentic 1940s backdrop. Every effort is made to ensure that all clothing is accurate, particularly military and police uniforms and hair stylists make sure that all waves and sweeps are as they would have been in wartime. Even the smallest accessories and props are chosen carefully, and real artefacts used where possible.

4.   A convoy of Foyle's War trucks and equipment comes into town during filming. Mobile dressing rooms, a make-up truck, equipment lorries and the catering vehicle all descend on the Old Town, transforming it into a real film set. Actors and crew all stay in local hotels and eat in local restaurants, really transforming the town into 'Foyle's Hastings' while filming goes on.

Houses Damaged by Night Raider

Houses were damaged when a high explosive bomb fell in a roadway in a residential district during a recent night raid on a South-East coast town.

Brothers Missing

F/O A. J. Crouch   Sgn. K. A. Crouch

Mr. and Mrs. H. E. Crouch, of 23, Horntye-road, St. Leonards, have received news that their son, Signalman K. A. Crouch, aged 21 years, is reported missing, believed killed, in Italy in June.

A member of Airborne Signals, he was attached to the 2/5th Army Air Support Control. Before the war he was on the staff of the Bexhill branch of the Midland Bank. He was an Old Hastonian.

Another son, Flying Officer A. J. Crouch, D.F.M., aged 23 years, failed to return from operations in May.

Gained His Wings

The many friends of Mr. Herbert A. Cordell, aged 24, of 48, Duke-road, Silverhill, St. Leonards, and formerly of Queen's - road, Hastings, will be pleased to learn that after training with the R.A.F. in South Africa he has gained his wings and is now Sergeant Pilot. He has been posted to the Middle East.

He attended Hastings Central School and was formerly a member of the Wellington-square Boys' Band of which his father, Mr. H. A. Cordell, was trainer and conductor.

Brief: Investigate life in Hastings during World War Two.

1.   With more than 550 High Explosive Bombs and 85 enemy air attacks, Hastings came under serious fire during the Second World War. The first of 85 enemy air attacks came on 26 July 1940 and the last on 2 August 1944.

2.   In the first attack, a single aircraft dropped 11 bombs, several of which fell on the cricket ground. Gloating German bombers returning from the raid claimed they'd made several successful hits on Hastings' harbour. Not quite the reality of what happened on the ground; damage was suffered, but most of it to a vacant cricket pitch.

3.   There was a disastrous attack on the town centre in September 1940. Significant damage was caused to Queens Road, Nelson Road, Milward Road and St Mary's Terrace. On 30 September, a bomb shattered the front of the Plaza cinema in Robertson Street. Eight people were killed instantly in this incident with four others dying later from their injuries.

4.   Thirty enemy planes rained death and destruction on Hastings in March 1943, unleashing around 25 powerful bombs on the town. The attack caused shocking devastation and significant loss of life. A total of 38 people were killed, 39 were seriously injured and 51 sustained minor injuries. Piles of rubble replaced several homes in the Silverhill area of the town, which suffered particularly terrible damage in the attack. Houses in Battle Road, Bury Road, Perth Road and Sedlescombe Road North suffered serious damage, and in Adelaide Road several homes were wrecked.

DO NOT BELIEVE RUMOURS AND DO NOT SPREAD THEM. WHEN YOU RECEIVE AN ORDER, MAKE QUITE SURE THAT IT IS A TRUE ORDER AND NOT A FAKED ORDER. MOST OF YOU KNOW YOUR POLICEMEN AND YOUR A.R.P. WARDENS BY SIGHT, YOU CAN TRUST THEM. IF YOU KEEP YOUR HEADS, YOU CAN ALSO TELL WHETHER A MILITARY OFFICER IS REALLY BRITISH OR ONLY PRETENDING TO BE SO. IF IN DOUBT ASK THE POLICE-MAN OR THE A.R.P. WARDEN. USE YOUR COMMON SENSE.

Killed in Action

Previously posted as "missing" Trooper G. Sanderson, of 35, Croft-road, Hastings, has now been reported killed in action in the Middle East on October 24th, 1942. Aged 25, Trooper Sanderson was a member of the Reconnaissance Corps. He was among those who served at Dunkirk.

His widow is now living in Salisbury.

"Strange Object" Exploded

SEDLESCOMBE BOY BADLY MUTILATED

The danger from strange objects found lying in the countryside was illustrated by a serious accident in the Sedlescombe district on Sunday, when a 12-year-old boy lost part of his left leg, right arm and right eye in an explosion.

The boy was Dennis Franks, of Yew Tree Cottage, Kent Street, Sedlescombe. He came across a small, unfamiliar object on some land in the neighbourhood. He took it home and it exploded in the backyard of his home. He was very severely mutilated. The St. John motor ambulance from Hastings was summoned and the boy was taken to the Royal East Sussex Hospital, where the lower part of his left leg and his right arm were amputated and his right eye had to be removed. He was also found to have received other injuries.

5. The people of Hastings suffered badly at the hands of the enemy, more than 150 locals lost their lives, 260 were left seriously injured and more than 440 others sustained minor injuries. More than 460 homes were destroyed, either by direct hit or as a result of damage suffered in attacks. German bombers hit Hastings with more than 550 High Explosive Bombs, 12 Oil Incendiary Bombs, 15 V1 flying bombs and 750 Small Incendiary Bombs.

6. Redevelopment in the Old Town was halted and large areas of the Old Town were abandoned as the war began to take its toll. Barbed wire, gun emplacements and tank traps blotted the seafront, replacing families and visitors enjoying the seaside. Fishermen got exceptional access to the beach, which was a 'no go' area. Risking their lives for their livelihoods, fishermen were in great danger going to sea during the war; three boats were lost in mine explosions.

7. Popular tourist attraction, St Clements Caves, became an air raid shelter, hospital and school, and was known to have housed 300 to 400 people. The network of underground tunnels served a much more practical purpose, giving shelter to many residents and becoming a permanent home to some whose homes had been destroyed. Life underground was not perfect, although bunk beds were provided and limited lighting strung up through the tunnels. Cave conditions put off some families, who preferred to take the risk in their own homes.

Hastings Man Killed

News has been received by Mr. and Mrs. T. G. Playford, of 17, St. Andrew's-square, that their youngest son, Sapper Reginald John Playford, R.E., who was serving in the Central Mediterranean Forces, has been killed on active service. Aged 23, Sapper Playford had been in the Middle East four and a half years and was due home shortly.

He joined the Territorial Army a month before the outbreak of war. Since then he had gained three Army certificates as a plumber.

Sapper Playford was educated at St. Mary-in-the-Castle School and sang in the St. Mary-in-the-Castle Church choir. He was employed as an apprentice by the Hastings Gas Company before joining the Army.

Mr. and Mrs. Playford have another son serving in India.

A score to settle

He's got something of the bull-dog,
He's as strong as any ox,
And he's used to freezing nights
And blazing sun.
He can give it — he can take it,
For he's learned to take hard knocks,
And he's got a score to settle
With the Hun.

Since the day that he was sworn in
As a very raw recruit,
He also swore he'd make
The Jerries run.
So pay homage to the soldier
And let's give him our salute,
For we've all a score to settle
With the Hun.

Maybe your son, your husband, brother or
sweetheart is out there. What can *you* do to help
him? What can all of us do to bring Victory
nearer? Just this—

SAVE MORE AND MORE.

Issued by the National Savings Committee

SHARP RAID ON S.E. COAST TOWN

Hotels and Public Houses Hit

Five public houses and two hotels
received direct hits in a rip-and-run day-
light raid on a S.E. Coast town on Sunday.

FORTUNATE ESCAPE

THE "BURMA ROAD"

RAID SERVICES PRAISED

Ruhr Dams Bombing

D.S.O. FOR HASTINGS OFFICER

These pictures show damage caused in Sunday's raid on a South-East Coast town: (1) What
remained of an antique shop. (2) A church had a narrow escape. (3) Searching the ruins
of a public house. (4) A residential hotel was another target. (5) More residential property.
(6) A restaurant building also suffered. (7) Damage in a shopping thoroughfare.
Wreckage of a public house and surrounding shops. (9) Shops and houses were damaged.
(10) Another residential "objective." (11) Shop premises hit.

"WINGS" WEEK TOTAL WAS £521,270

Fine Rally By Small Savers

Hastings easily reached the half-
million mark during the "Wings for
Victory" Week, which ended on Saturday.

AREA TOTALS

SCHOOLS PART

Posthumous Medals For Gallantry

AWARDS TO HASTINGS LIFEBOATMEN

North Africa Casualty

In Japanese Hands

★ Savings
are an important part
of the
WAR EFFORT

Further evidence

Page 24

8.   The Old Town suffered its worst attack on 23 May 1943 when the Swan Inn in the High Street was destroyed. It was a busy Sunday lunchtime when 16 people were killed in the attack, which also destroyed, 1,2 and 3 Swan Terrace. Residents could not believe the devastation on this quiet Sunday afternoon, the bomb damage completely changed the landscape. A plaque now stands on the site of the Swan Inn in memory of those who lost their lives that day.

9.   Despite searching through the night and the following day, rescuers only recovered one man and a dog alive in the rubble. In the same 1943 attack, four other public houses and two hotels were struck, killing a total of 30 Hastings people. Seafront landmarks The Albany Hotel and Queens Hotel were also hit, and awful damage inflicted on surrounding houses and shops.

10.   Relief swept across Hastings in 1944. August that year saw the beach crammed with bathers after being reopened and in November residents heard the final air raid siren. Shortly after St Clements Caves was reopened as a visitor attraction after four years as an air raid shelter. Familiar elements of life before the war were returning one by one, reassuring the residents that their nightmare was over.

"End Will Be Quick— When It Comes"

Hastings & St. Leonards O

No. 6401   Registered at the General Post Office as a Newspaper   TELEPHONE... 1167 (3 lines) Extensions to all Departments

SATURDAY, JANUARY 15, 1944   POSTAGE THREE-HALFPENCE

RATEPAYERS' FINE ACHIEVEMENT

...uncil Tribute

...ands, Hastings Town ...New Year well by ...necting on Tuesday ...hour. Commenting ...rer's report, Alder-...(chairman of the ...id a high tribute to ...rers.

...COUNCIL IN ...COMMITTEE

...WAR WAGE INCREASE

Home Guards' Annual Dinner

The annual dinner of 2111 Company, West Kent Home Guard Transport Column was held at the Ritz Cafe on Saturday.

D.F.M. for Hastings Man

The Distinguished Fl... Medal has been awarded ... Sergt. Charles Leslie ... R.A.F., husband of Mrs...

Call To Youth To Enrol In Messenger Pool

SQUADRON-LDR. LEAROYD, V.C., AT TO-MORROW'S RALLY

THE Town Clerk's appeal in our last week's issue to the youth of Hastings will, we are certain, receive the whole-hearted support it deserves...

Seaman Missing

Mr. and Mrs. W. Betts, of 93, Saxon-road, Hastings, have this week received news from the Admiralty that their younger son, Leading Seaman Frederick "Bunny" Betts, is missing since drowned. His brother, Flight-Sergt. Thomas Betts, R.A.F. has been missing since August, 1942.

Only 21 years of age, Leading Seaman Betts volunteered for the Navy in 1939 as soon as he was old enough...

A First Prize for Hastings

POTATO DISPLAY

First prize in the south-east divisional area in the potato display contest run in connection with the Hastings Potato Week in the early part of last year has been awarded to Messrs. A. K. Ford, of Queen's-avenue, Hastings...

Military Post... Police

MR. A. G. CARGILL, Assistant Chief Constable of the Hastings Force, has been called special military duties and posted as Lieut.-Colonel...

...Leonards Observer

...RCH 11, 1944   POSTAGE THREE-HALFPENCE   Price THREEPENCE

...ARDS PIER...

Police Chief to Retire

SUPT. BUDDLE'S CAREER

Brothers Meet in Italy

Save Water to Save Fuel

COUNCIL WARNING AGAINST WASTE

Drug Tablets Returned

FINDER SAW APPEAL IN "OBSERVER"

Reported Missing

Airman Missing

L.L.K. Gives Away £160

RECORD YEAR FOR "OBSERVER" CHILDREN'S LEAGUE

1943 was a record year for to make an extra donation to the L.L.K. Farthing...

Warship Week Sequel

NEXT WEEK'S CEREMONY

Next Wednesday at 3 p.m. at the White Rock Pavilion (Great Hall), Vice-Admiral E. J. Hardman-Jones will hand over to the borough a shield from H.M.S. Hastings in commemoration of Hastings' War savings effort in Warship Week, 1942.

Transferred to Germany

A letter card received on Saturday by Mr. and Mrs. C. J. Sendall of ...road North...

D.S.M. for Local Seaman

'A cup of tea'

D.S.M. for Local Seaman

ver

Price THREEPENCE

TAL RESORTS' ONDITION

ert Gower Visits Hastings

HASTINGS was visited yesterday (Friday) by Sir Robert Gower M.P. for Gillingham, chairman of the Committee of Members of Parliament representing the defence and evacuation areas.

He accepted an invitation from the Mayor (Alderman Dr. W. E. Jameson, J.P.) to lunch at Summer Fields and to meet a number of prominent citizens of the borough.

The "Observer" understands that his visit was entirely unofficial, but Sir Robert took the opportunity of discussing with the Mayor and the other guests he met the conditions produced by the war which have vitally affected the coastal resorts, including Hastings and St. Leonards.

It is understood that he indicated that his committee propose to press the Government to set up the Departmental Committee of Inquiry asked for by the notice of motion standing on the Order Paper of the House of Commons.

Sir Robert paid a high tribute to the work done on the committee by Mr Maurice Hely-Hutchinson, the Borough Member, who had, he declared, applied himself energetically to all the matters coming within the scope of its operations.

He congratulated the borough upon having so able and energetic a business man to represent it in the House of Commons.

The terms of the Commons' motion are: "That in the opinion of this House it is desirable that a Departmental Committee should be appointed to consider the position of the Defence and Evacuation Areas, and to report as to what steps are necessary or desirable for the alleviation of present hardships and for the reinstatement of the means of livelihood of the population of these areas."

Gallant Sussex Officer

For gallant and distinguished services in Italy, Brigadier L. G. Whistler, Royal Sussex Regiment, has been awarded a second bar to his D.S.O.

Brigadier Whistler was adjutant of Hastings Territorial Unit of the Royal Sussex Regiment from 1929 to 1932.

s Guard

Sergt. Cyril ... utland, Royal Sussex ... member of a guard for the Royal ... ived by Mrs. Putland from her ... with the King. Sergt. Putland ... e guard.

USE

Doing Their Bit

...ver R. J. Potter, ... 20, Silverhill, ...-road, Guestling

P.S.M. J. T. Hayler, aged 43, 164, Old Lane, Hollington.

Pte. C. M. Mitchell, aged ..., Vicarage-road.

Pte. J. Adams, aged 20, 75, Emmanuel-road.

Stoker W. Muzzell aged 20, 161, Bexhill-road, St. Leonards.

Bdr. J. F. H. Hazzard, 36, Silchester-road, St. Leonards.

Sapper J. Cossom, aged 18, 77, The Ridge.

Seaman J. S. Edwards, aged 20, 5a, York-buildings.

Pte. Cecil Bursen, 9, Coburg-place.

Stoker 1st Class Fred Butchers, aged 20, 10, Cliftonville-road, St. Leonards.

A.C.1 A. Whiteman, 37, Percy-road, Ore.

Sapper E. Jinks, aged 40, 55, Elphinstone-road.

A/A. S. G. Funnell, aged 16, 2, Hill-street.

Pte. A. S. Funnell, aged 28, 2, Hill-street.

Pte. C. R. Mepham, aged 20, 31, Vicarage-road.

Pte. Richard Brann, aged 21, 26, Grove-road, Ore.

Pte. A. G. Hutchinson, 7, Fellows-road.

Rfn. W. Cossom, aged 23, 35, St. George's-road.

Sapper W. H. Phillips, 156, Parker-road.

L/Sgt. V. Hutchinson, aged 30, 3, Lewis-road, Hollington.

Seaman F. Whiteman, 497, Bexhill-road, St. Leonards.

Driver E. H. Thomas, aged 31, 8a, Middle-street.

Driver F. C. Pascoe, aged 27, 31, Southwater-road, St. Leonards.

Noah Lee, aged 24, 60, Quebec-road, Hollington.

Tptr. R. S. Thornton, aged 15, 27, Pevensey-road, St. Leonards.

Pte. E. L. Evans, aged 17, Pebsham-lane, Bexhill-road, St. Leonards.

Cpl. W. Barham, 68, Quebec-road, Hollington.

L/Cpl. L. F. Huntly aged 21, 32, Manor-road.

L/Cpl. J. Pickford, aged 30, 44, St. Paul's-road, St. Leonards.

Sgt. F. Stonham, aged 25, 3, Battle-hill, Battle.

Gnr. Fitter E. A. Morris, aged 27, 35, Carisbrooke-road, St. Leonards.

Pte. F. Bell, aged 32, 37, Beauchamp-road, Hollington.

L.A.C. G. Spilstead, aged 20, 194, St. Helen's-road.

Pte. E. Eaton, aged 21, 66, Church-road, St. Leonards.

L/Cpl. H. Bean, aged 29, 23, Adelaide-road, Hollington.

L/Bdr. R. W. Thornton, aged 22, 1, Station-road.

L/Cpl. A. Dunk, aged 39, 29, Bohemia-road, St. Leonards.

... Breeds, aged 22, ..., Bembrook-road

Pte. C. T. Goldsmith, aged 30, 10, Waterworks-road.

A.C.1 E. L. Martin, aged 21, 83, Bulverhythe-road, St. Leonards.

Gnr. T. J. Avery, aged 17, 142, Mount Pleasant-road.

M. A. Cresswell, aged 22, 44, St. Paul's-road, St. Leonards.

Signlr. W. Pickford, aged ..., 44, St. Paul's-road, St. Leonards.

...river J. Downs, ...ed 35, 12a, Ar...-road, St. Leonards.

Pte. H. Barton, aged 19, 36, Ormerod-avenue, Hollington.

Driver D. H. White, aged 23, 11, St. Paul's-road, St. Leonards.

O/S. J. Blackman, aged 21, 12a, Hill-street.

Pte. D. Smith, 55, Quebec-road, Hollington.

Gnr. J. H. Thornton, aged 27, Bohemia-road, St. Leonards.

...btained on application to the "Observer" Office, Hastings.

OIL BLAZE CAUSED HOLLINGTON FIRE

Inquest Story of Christmas Day Tragedy

Because she was in a hurry to go to an early church service with her family, a mother tried to re-light a smouldering sitting-room fire in a Hollington bungalow with rags dipped in paraffin, and through the can of oil catching alight the bungalow was set ablaze.

This was disclosed at the inquest at Hastings on Monday on William Price (37), builder, of 1, Coventry-road, Hollington Old Lane, and his son Francis ("Robin") Price, aged two years and nine months, who lost their lives in a fire which badly damaged their home on Christmas Day.

A verdict of "Death by misadventure" was recorded by the Borough Coroner (Mr. H. C. Davenport Jones).

LOCATIONS OF BOMBS DROPPED OVER HASTINGS.

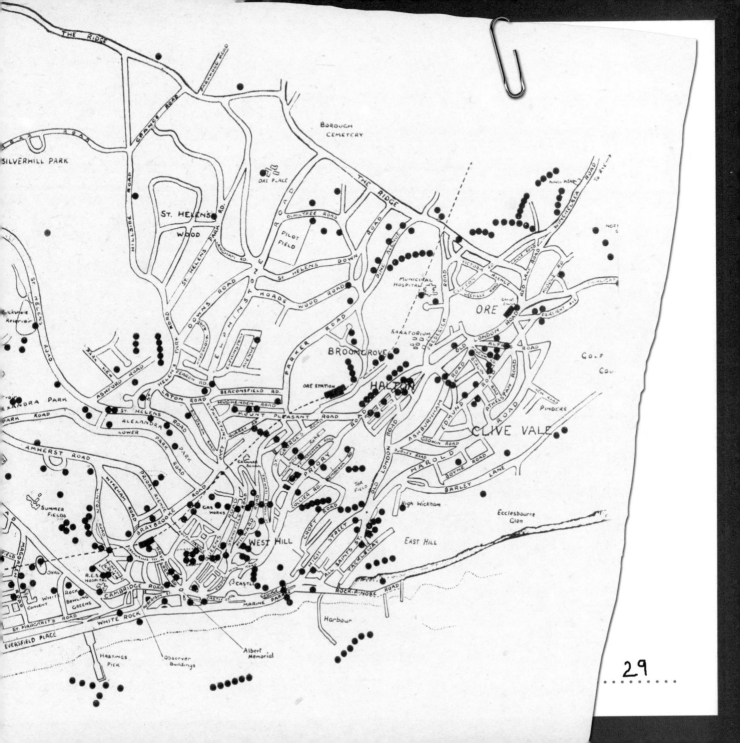

29

Crime, evacuees, the Home Guard and Dunkirk are all explored in episodes of Foyle's War. This section takes a look at how the reality in Hastings compared with the fiction of the show.

Home Guard

1.   In the series two episode 'War Games', DCS Foyle referees a large-scale exercise for the Home Guard. During the manoeuvre, a tradesman protecting his links with the Nazis shoots a member of the Home Guard, leaving Foyle to investigate. The Home Guard played an important role in wartime Hastings, providing protection from invaders as well as improving morale and the feeling of safety.

2.   The Local Defence Volunteers, which became the Home Guard, was formed in May 1940 when a radio appeal for volunteers was broadcast. With the heightened fear of German invasion more than 800 local men, most of them veterans, stepped up. Volunteers also included those who were too young, too old, the infirm and those whose civilian jobs were vital to the war effort. Women were not allowed to join any combative unit, so they were excluded from the Home Guard. However, the Women's Home Guard Auxiliaries later worked alongside the male volunteers, performing administrative duties.

3.   The Home Guard was then issued with uniforms and whatever weapons could be found. Most of these were from the First World War, or were make-do items from personal collections, and even household tools in certain cases. Affectionately termed the 'Dad's Army', the Home Guard had a reputation for being poorly equipped and a little disorganised. Despite some early inadequacies, the Home Guard volunteers still made a valuable contribution to the war effort.

4.   As the war continued the Home Guard played a pivotal role defending Hastings. Members were on duty every fourth night, patrolling the town for suspicious activity. The volunteers were particularly on high alert for parachute invasions. The Home Guard was based at headquarters in Sedlescombe Road, and patrolled as far as Bexhill Road and Hollington. In 1942, the Home Guard became involved in a mock invasion coordinated by the police, the local authority and the military. The exercise was designed to test communications between vital services in the town in the event of an invasion.

5.   The Home Guard stood down in Hastings in 1944, when more than 500 members of the 23rd Batallion Sussex Home Guard gathered to officially disband. The streets were lined with members of the public, who gathered to show appreciation to the 'Dad's Army'.

Crime

1.   Crime keeps Foyle at home in the South East during the Second World War and his investigations keep viewers glued to Foyle's War. Although, perhaps, not to the extent seen in the television show, crime and disorder were also features of real wartime Hastings.

2.   Despite the distractions of war abroad, those left in Hastings did not refrain completely from criminal activity, and the police and courts were faced with a range of law-breaking behaviour. Murder is a recurring theme in several episodes, with Foyle often finding himself at the heart of complex investigations. In series one DCS Foyle investigated a stabbed body found after a bombing raid. In series two the death of a member of the Home Guard sparked questioning, as did the murder of a town councillor. Murder continues in series three when the son of an MI5 agent is found dead and a farmer is killed on his land in another episode. Series four deaths include a fire victim and a war hero and in series five, a woman dies at a munitions factory leaving Foyle to get to the truth.

3.   In wartime Hastings there was actually only one murder recorded, in September 1941. The killing of a 74-year-old woman in Carlisle Parade underground car park was followed by the suicide of her killer, a 23-year-old Army Private. During the war the car park was used as a public air raid shelter, military accommodation and as a base for local emergency services. The victim, was known to sleep in the underground car park after being bombed out of her home. After hearing the case in Court, the jury decided that the killer must have been of unsound mind.

ESSENTIAL WORKERS MUST STAY, *particularly the following classes—*

THE HOME GUARD.   OBSERVER CORPS.
COASTGUARDS, COAST WATCHERS AND LIFEBOAT CREWS.
POLICE AND SPECIAL CONSTABULARY.
FIRE BRIGADE AND AUXILIARY FIRE SERVICE.
A.R.P. AND CASUALTY SERVICES.
MEMBERS OF LOCAL AUTHORITIES AND THEIR OFFICIALS AND EMPLOYEES.
WORKERS ON THE LAND.
PERSONS ENGAGED ON WAR WORK, AND OTHER ESSENTIAL SERVICES.
PERSONS EMPLOYED BY CONTRACTORS ON DEFENCE WORK.
... WATERAGE, GAS AND ELECTRICITY UNDERTAKINGS.
... ND DISTRIBUTION OF FOOD.
... T TRADES.
... D CHEMISTS.
... LIGION.
... PLOYEES.
... BANKS.
... DERTAKINGS, NAMELY
... S, AND ROAD TRANSPORT
... ND GOODS).

CHECKED
24 HR. SHEET   34   LEAVE THIS SPACE BLANK

Name VICTOR HENDLEBY
Alias THE LOOTER

Classification HIGHLY CONFIDENTIAL
Ref. HEAD OF ORGANISED CRIME

No. X5239417   Sex MALE

1.—Right Thumb	2.—R. Index Finger	3.—R. Middle Finger	4.—R. Ring Finger	5.—R. Little Finger
6.—Left Thumb	7.—L. Index Finger	8.—L. Middle Finger	9.—L. Ring Finger	10.—L. Little Finger

Four fingers taken simultaneously
Left hand

12 MONTHS

Left Thumb | Right Thumb

Four fingers taken simultaneously
Right hand

Exhibit A
Proof of
Identification

4.   Foyle is also called to investigate organised looting in the series two episode 'Fifty Ships'. There were a number of reported cases in Hastings during the war. Bombed houses and houses left empty by evacuees were attractive targets for looters in Hastings, with cases even reported during air raids.

5.   An interesting case came to light in 1941 when a 20-year-old man gained illegal entry into a house after the occupant had been evacuated. The house contents were sold onto to a second-hand dealer, who turned out to be an organised looter, making a healthy living from the crime. Both cases were heard at Hastings Magistrates Court, where the dealer was sentenced to 12 months' hard labour and the young man to three months. These culprits were lucky as looting was officially punishable with death during the Second World War, although such a harsh punishment was never actually given.

DO NOT GIVE ANY GERMAN ANYTHING. DO NOT TELL HIM ANYTHING. HIDE YOUR FOOD AND YOUR BICYCLES. HIDE YOUR MAPS. SEE THAT THE ENEMY GETS NO PETROL. IF YOU HAVE A CAR OR MOTOR BICYCLE, PUT IT OUT OF ACTION WHEN NOT IN USE. IT IS NOT ENOUGH TO REMOVE THE IGNITION KEY; YOU MUST MAKE IT USELESS TO ANYONE EXCEPT YOURSELF.

IF YOU ARE A GARAGE PROPRIETOR, YOU MUST WORK OUT A PLAN TO PROTECT YOUR STOCK OF PETROL AND YOUR CUSTOMERS' CARS. REMEMBER THAT TRANSPORT AND PETROL WILL BE THE INVADER'S MAIN DIFFICULTIES. MAKE SURE THAT NO INVADER WILL BE ABLE TO GET HOLD OF YOUR CARS, PETROL, MAPS OR BICYCLES.

Dunkirk

1.   Extraordinary times demand extraordinary solutions and, at the climax of the series one episode 'The White Feather', viewers get a glimpse of the events at Dunkirk as some of the stranded Allied soldiers are brought ashore during history's most daring naval rescue effort.

2.   On Monday 26 May 1940, any shallow-draught vessel capable of getting to Dover was called in to take advantage of Hitler's baffling decision to halt the advance of his Panzer Divisions just short of Dunkirk. This unexpected flaw in Nazi military planning gave naval commanders a narrow window of opportunity to execute a partial evacuation of Allied soldiers from the unforgiving Dunkirk beaches.

3.   On Saturday 30 May 1940, 10 Hastings fishing boats, the Hastings lifeboat 'The Cyril and Lilian Bishop' and the fireboat joined the rag-tag fleet of little vessels to help the Navy save hundreds of thousands of lives. In the end, only the lifeboat actually made it to Dunkirk and, although coxswain George Moon and his crew were more than prepared to make the dangerous trip, they were sent home by train from Dover when the Navy commandeered the boat there.

4.   This was because the crew of the Hythe Lifeboat apparently refused to make the crossing, believing that more lives would be lost if their lifeboat was destroyed. With no time for negotiation or persuasion, the Navy wrongly assumed that all crews would behave in the same way and sent all of them home. George Moon was unfairly branded a coward on his return to the town, and this is said to have troubled him for many years after. Hastings Lifeboat survived the ordeal albeit with superficial shrapnel damage. Ironically of the numerous lifeboats involved in the rescue, only one failed to return – Hythe's.

5.   As Hitler became aware of the Allies' plans, Hastings resident Ronald Parish was one of the few men who stayed behind in Dunkirk to fight a rearguard action against the advancing Panzer Divisions. He was captured and held prisoner for four years in Germany. The bravery and selflessness of a young man from a small south coast town helped 333,226 British, French and Belgian soldiers escape and live on to fight another day.

The Allied victory in the war is a vast tapestry made from such tiny sacrifices.

Evacuations

1.   In the series five episode 'Casualties of War', Foyle's life is turned upside down when his goddaughter Lydia and her seven-year-old son James turn up on his doorstep needing somewhere to stay. James has been severely traumatised by a bombing at his London school where most of his classmates and teachers were killed.

2.   For nine months between 1939 and 1940, countless children from London made Hastings their temporary home. For many it was their first experience of the seaside but the holiday atmosphere soon changed when Hastings became part of the south coast's 'Defence Area'. This 20 mile-wide strip of land with mined beaches, roadblocks and curfews was not exactly a safe haven for evacuees and so the town's big city guests were immediately moved. It wasn't long before evacuation plans were drawn up for the town's own schoolchildren who would be in the firing line of any German invasion.

3.   On Sunday 21 July 1940, some five days before the first enemy air attack. Half of the town's school children were evacuated to safe reception areas in Hertfordshire and Bedfordshire. All schools were closed with immediate effect and the town's status changed from a "reception area" to an "evacuation area".

WHY EVACUATION?

There are still a number of people who ask "What is the need for all this business about evacuation? Surely if war comes it would be better for families to stick together and not go breaking up their homes?"

It is quite easy to understand this feeling, because it is difficult for us in this country to realise what war in these days might mean. If we were involved in war, our big cities might be subjected to determined attacks from the air—at any rate in the early stages—and although our defences are strong and are rapidly growing stronger, some bombers would undoubtedly get through.

We must see to it then that the enemy does not secure his chief objects—the creation of anything like panic, or the crippling dislocation of our civil life.

One of the first measures we can take to prevent this is the removal of the children from the more dangerous areas.

Exhibit B

4.   When the remainder of the town's school children were evacuated by rail, parents were asked not to attend because of fears over congestion and people's natural unwillingness to let their children go to various unknown destinations around the country. This was almost universally ignored and, in a day of terrible upheaval and turmoil, children were given a blank postcard so that they could write home as soon as they arrived and give parents their new temporary address.

5.   The 280 pupils of the Hastings Grammar School were sent to St. Albans where they were given a chocolate bar and taken off in groups to be sorted. Ironically for the children of a resort town where visitors were always welcome, some people refused to take the evacuees and police were brought in to enforce the order.

6.   The evacuation experience was remarkable in its diversity. There were some instances of horrendous abuse and neglect but many children found warm welcomes and forged friendships that outlasted the war and endure to this day.

Thrusting the Chin into the Civilian Respirator.

Adjusting the Civilian Respirator.

SATURDAY, OCTOBER 30, 1943

HASTINGS MEN BACK FROM GERMANY

Homecoming Eagerly Awaited This Week

STAFF-SERGEANT'S STORY OF HIS EXPERIENCES

Nowhere has the return of the repatriated British prisoners of war, who reached this country from Germany this week, been more eagerly awaited than it has in Hastings, where several homes recently received the official War Office notification that husbands or sons were among the men chosen for exchange.

ALREADY one N.C.O. Staff-Sergeant, John Huggins, of St. Orville-road, has reached his home, and several other men have been expected for some days.

Staff-Sergeant Huggins, in respect of whom consolation is known to have... Louis Frank... Minnie Court...

NEIGHBOURS WELCOME

Captain Trower

Captain G. S. Trower, R.A.M.C., son of the late Dr. and Mrs. Trower, of St. Helen's-road, St. Leonards, has also been repatriated. He arrived in this country on Tuesday. He had been a prisoner since Dunkirk.

Neighbours gave Staff-Sergeant Huggins a rousing welcome home

Stepped in Front

Poppy Day Appeal

CALL FOR EMBLEM SELLERS

We have received the following letter:—

AIM AT £1,066

The following sum has been... sent to Mrs. M. Bird...

St. Leonards Man Missing

News has been received by Mrs. F. Baxley, of 8, Tower-road, St. Leonards, that her husband, L.-Cpl. Norman John Baxley...

A.A Guns, Sea Road

Anthony Horowitz

Series creator and writer

How do you find filming in Hastings?

I always enjoy coming here. We've actually returned for all five seasons – and it's never rained!

Have you worked with any co-writers on the show?

I've written most of the 16 two-hour slots that we've made, but I did collaborate with other writers on a couple of them. Only two episodes will have been completely written by other writers.

Any particular reason for that?

It's always difficult bringing new talent into a long-running series and it has to be said that Foyle's War is extremely demanding. You need a pretty good knowledge of the Second World War, an understanding of all the different characters and the ability to construct a workable murder/mystery. In the end, the producers found it easier to keep coming back to me.

How do you decide which wartime issues to focus on? Have you been influenced by any memories/stories given to you by your family?

Most of the stories come from my extensive reading. Many of them – American GIs, Dunkirk, evacuees etc – screamed out for attention.

What attracted you to write about the American GIs?

Pearl Harbour and the American entry into the war was one of the main turning points. The GIs arrived in their thousands – the first real invasion of Great Britain since the Normans…which is something the people of Hastings would know all about! That's why we called the episode "Invasion".

Is it difficult to find a balance between an accurate representation of the 1940s and the demands of a modern audience?

We try to make everything, from the cars to the costumes, to the characters, as authentic as possible. At the same time, because we have such strong stories with murder at their heart, a modern audience is drawn in. At least, that's what I hope.

How do you and Michael Kitchen work together?

We were extremely fortunate to be able to cast Michael – who was our first choice for the part. Over the years we have developed the character together although he can be very demanding.

Really?

I mean that in the best possible way. He is an actor who won't say a line unless he believes it totally and we often work through scenes word by word.

Do you have much of a say in how the scenes are shot? Are you there on set?

Unfortunately, I can't be on set all the time…and anyway, it isn't my job. Don't forget that there are at least ninety people involved in the production and once the script has left my hands, I just let them get on with it. I should add that being married to the producer does give me a slight advantage, though!

On writing, how often do you re-write an episode before it feels right? Do you get writer's block and if so, how do you overcome it? Do you get the urge to change things when filming has started?

I write a first draft. Then I get notes from the producer, director, the script editor and the Imperial War Museum. A lot of notes! But they all have to be dealt with and I'll probably write four or five drafts before we start shooting. If I do any more than that, it's a sign that something has gone badly wrong.

Left: Author Victoria Seymour
Middle: Charles Banks, Ex-Hastings Police, WWII
Right: Mrs Jean Gill, junior police clerk during the 1940s

Charles Banks, Ex-Hastings Police, WWII

Charles ('Charlie') Banks was almost a real-life Foyle, being a sergeant and then an inspector in the Hastings Borough Police Force. Charlie was based at Hastings Central Police Station, part of the Town Hall. He was the last surviving member of the Hastings Borough Police Force to have joined before the end of World War Two.

Charlie sadly passed away in January 2009, but visited the Town Hall before he died, and reminisced about the war.

He was always quick to point out any historical inaccuracies which might threaten to appear in the show, but said...

"The show is very realistic, very well done and, I think, a true record. But they revive often painful memories. With many of these bombing incidents there were a number of casualties, some of them very severely mutilated and it was quite a gruesome experience. But it went on so long that we got hardened to it and handled it as just part of the job."

His obituary by Richard Morris in the Hastings Observer following his death at the age of 95 summed his life up :- "Whether dodging bombs during air raids, chasing after drunk Canadian soldiers, solving murders or keeping one step ahead of the wartime black market, Mr Banks served his community with a dogged determination.

"Not only was Charles Banks' life a remarkable one, but the streets of Hastings were a safer place as a result of it."

INVESTIGATION DEPARTMENT: Eye Witness Accounts

Carol Boorman, Wartime Croft Road Resident

Carol Boorman (nee Breach) was born in 13 Croft Road, just a few doors from DCS Foyle's fictional home at no 31, before WWII broke out, and lived in Croft Road at the start of the war, moving during the war to The Croft, just around the corner. She still lives in the Old Town of Hastings now.

Left: 13 Croft Road c1940 with Caroline (Bess) Breach
Right: 13 Croft Road 2010 with Carol Boorman (nee Breach), Bess's daughter

"I was very young when war broke out, but still have vivid memories of it. In particular I remember being told not to touch anything I saw laying in the street, in case it was unexploded ammunition, or even a bomb. My Dad was an ARP Warden, so was kept very busy.

"I went to the Cavendish School, underneath St Clement's Church Hall in Croft Road, which can be seen in many of the Foyle's War episodes, and that brings back a lot of memories.

"The Dunkirk Evacuation episode was very close to home for me. I come from a fishing family, and my Mum's my Uncle George (George Moon) was cox of the Hastings Lifeboat at the time.

"I spent a lot of time in St Clement's Caves too, both sleeping and going to school there. It's a shame they couldn't have set a scene there too, although 'the Caves' have changed beyond recognition now.

"I do enjoy watching the filming of Foyle's War, as although there is obviously artistic licence, they certainly recreate the atmosphere of wartime in Hastings Old Town."

51

Foyle's War Merchandise

Subject.........

Evidence

....

....

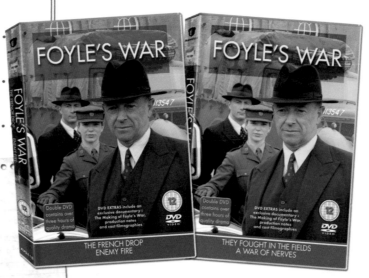

Available on
DVD and VHS
from all good retailers

Official Foyle's War
merchandise available at
local stockists or can be
found online.

The Foyle's War soundtrack
is available on CD
from all good retailers

Page.....52.....

greenlit

www.greenlit.co.uk

For information about accommodation, local attractions and much more visit:

Hastings Information Centre
Priory Meadow
Queens Square
Hastings
TN34 1TL

Call 01424 451111

Log on to **www.visit1066country.com** for more pictures of Foyle's War filming and also for accommodation, events and entertainment listings.

Fans of Foyle's War may be interested in the range of WWII exhibits on show at:

Hastings Old Town Hall Museum
High Street
Hastings
TN34 1EW

Additional Reading

The following publications are all available from Hastings Information Centre.

Victory's Children
By Victoria Seymour
£9.99

Letters from Lavender Cottage
Hastings in WWII and Austerity
By Victoria Seymour
£9.99

Court in the Act
By Victoria Seymour
£9.99